MAPS AND MAP-MAKING

FACTS ● THINGS TO MAKE ● ACTIVITIES

ANITA GANERI
Illustrated by Raymond Turvey

Watts Books
London ● New York ● Sydney

WARNING
You will need a sharp knife for some
of the projects in this book. Ask an
adult to help you and be very careful.
Always cut on a board when you are
using a knife or a saw.

© Watts Books 1995

Watts Books
96 Leonard Street
London EC2A 4RH

Franklin Watts
14 Mars Road
Lane Cove
NSW 2066

UK ISBN: 0 7496 1869 8
Dewey Classification Number: 526

10 9 8 7 6 5 4 3 2 1

Editor: Annabel Martin
Consultant: Olive Pearson
Designed by: Sally Boothroyd
Photography by: Martyn Chillmaid
Additional picture research by: Veneta Bullen

A CIP catalogue record for this book is available from
the British Library.

Printed in the United Kingdom

CONTENTS

WHAT IS A MAP?

A map is a picture of the world around us. There are many different types of map. One map might show the streets and landmarks in our local town. Another might show what the landscape is like for a whole country. Another might show the weather forecast for a whole continent.

STREET PLANS

A street plan is a map of the streets and buildings in a town or city. It shows the names of the streets, the names of different parts of the city, and railway and bus stations. Street maps also show certain buildings that people might want to find, such as the library or police station.

BOOK OF MAPS

An atlas is a book of maps. A world atlas contains topographic maps of every country in the world, showing towns and cities, rivers and mountains, major roads and railways. It might also contain thematic maps, showing other things about the countries, such as what the climate is like or what crops are grown.

Street plan

Atlas showing physical map (below)

SPECIAL MAPS

Not all maps show areas of the Earth's surface. There are many special types of map. For example, oceanographers use maps of the sea bottom, geologists use maps of the rocks under the ground, and astronomers use maps of the night sky and of the Moon.

MAKING MAPS

Making and studying maps is called cartography. To make a map, you need information about where things are and how big they are. For maps of small areas like your school, things can be measured and drawn by hand. Maps of large areas contain a huge amount of information. Measurements are taken from photographs and satellite images and stored on a computer.

Moon map (above)

Satellite image of Earth (below)

MAKING PLANS

A plan is a map of quite a small area, such as a room, a school, a shopping centre or the streets of a town centre. A plan shows where things are so it is easy to find them.

SYMBOLS AND KEYS

Different buildings and types of ground are shown on the plan in different colours. Objects such as trees and fences are shown by small pictures or shapes, which are called symbols. A person using the plan needs to know what the colours, lines and symbols mean, so a plan or map always has a key.

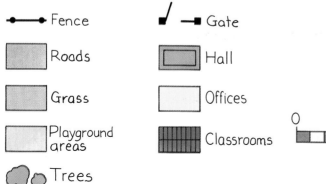

SCALE

Plans and maps are much smaller than the actual objects, areas and distances that they show. In the plan shown here, an object one metre long in real life is drawn 1 mm long on the plan. The scale is 1mm = 1m (1:1000). This can also be shown by a line called a scale bar. You can use the scale to work out real life sizes and distances.

DRAWING A PLAN

Try making a simple plan of your classroom or bedroom. You need to collect the information, decide what scale to use, then draw the plan. Finally, add a key and draw the scale on.

▲ **1.** Start by measuring the sides of your room. Now decide what scale to use. Try a scale of 1:20 – 1 cm on the plan equals 20 cm in the room. So if one side of the room is 400 cm (4 m) long, it will be 20 cm long on the plan. Draw the sides of the room on your paper.

Try making coloured shapes for the objects. Draw a plan of each object to scale and cut it out. Now you can use the plan to try fitting the things into your room in a different way.

▲ **2.** Now measure the position and size of the bed, table and cupboards in your room. Draw them on the plan at the correct scale.

SYMBOLS AND SIZES

The information on a map is shown by lines, colours and symbols. Symbols are small pictures or shapes which show small things on the ground, such as trees, churches, electricity pylons and so on. The meaning of all the symbols is shown in the key. Most maps also have a scale so that you can work out distances from the map. A grid helps you to find places on the map quickly.

ROADS AND RAILWAYS

Roads are shown as lines. Different colours are used for different types of road – one colour for motorways, another for main roads, and another for minor roads.

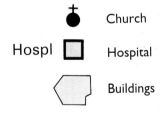

Main Road

Minor Road

BUILDINGS

Buildings are shown as blocks of colour. Important buildings such as churches, police stations and hospitals are shown with small symbols or letters.

✝ Church

Hospl ☐ Hospital

⬠ Buildings

HOW FAR?

Maps of small areas which have a lot of detail, such as town plans, are called large-scale maps. Maps of large areas with less detail, such as maps of a country, are called small-scale maps. Every map has a scale so that you can work out how far it is from one place to another on the map.

Small-scale map

Large-scale map **MEXICO CITY**

NATURAL FEATURES

Symbols and colours show what the ground is like. Tree symbols show woods. Blue lines show streams and rivers. The way the ground goes up and down to make hills and valleys is shown by shading or lines called contour lines. Contour lines are imaginary lines which join points which are the same height above sea level.

  Rivers

  Woodland

WHERE ON THE MAP?

A grid system is used to help find places on a map. Some maps use a simple grid with letters and numbers. Others use a grid like a graph. An accurate position can be given by saying how far across and up the map the point is. You can find out how to use grids on page 25.

STRING MEASURER

You can measure distances on a map very easily using a piece of string.

▲ **1.** Lay a piece of string along the scale line on the map with one end of the string at the zero mark. At each division on the scale, make a mark on the string. Use different colours for large and small divisions.

2. To find the distance between two places, lay the string along the roads that you would have to go along. Count the divisions along the string to find the distance.

You can use the string measurer with any map that has the same scale.

9

MAKING MAPS

Before a map can be drawn, all of the information needed (called data) must be gathered together. The data is made up of measurements and other information, for example, what buildings are used for, what sorts of trees are in a wood, or where the ground is boggy. Once all the data is collected the map can be drawn.

MEASURING THE GROUND

The data for large-scale, local maps and plans is gathered by measuring the ground. A surveyor starts at one point (such as a gate post or the corner of a building) and measures the position of other points from it. For small, simple plans, the surveyor needs only a tape measure. For plans and maps of larger areas, special instruments are used. A theodolite is used to measure angles accurately. Electronic measuring devices use an infra-red light beam to measure distances accurately.

PHOTOGRAPHY FROM THE SKY

The data for small-scale maps comes from photographs taken from aeroplanes or space satellites above the area to be mapped. They are called aerial photographs. Lots of photographs are needed to cover a large area. The size and position of things can be measured from the photographs once they have been adjusted to account for distortions. Photographs also show what the land is being used for. Special satellite photographs can show up details of different types of vegetation on the ground.

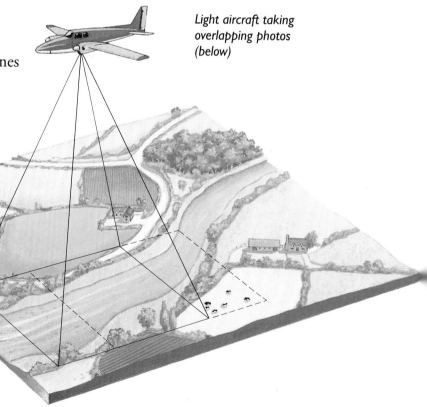

Light aircraft taking overlapping photos (below)

STEREOSCOPIC VIEWING

If two photographs are taken from slightly different positions and looked at in a special viewer, the landscape can be seen in three dimensions. Hills and tall buildings seem to leap out of the picture. These photographs are called stereo photographs or stereo pairs. They are used to measure distances, sizes, and the height of the land.

Look at the pictures through two cardboard tubes – one for each eye. The pictures will merge to give a 3-D effect.

DRAWING A MAP

Once all the information has been gathered, the map can be drawn. Maps and plans used to be drawn in pen and ink but today they can be drawn by computer too. The computer uses data stored in it to draw different types of map, such as a street plan, a road map or a map of places to visit.

Information from a map being added into the computer.

11

MAKE A TREASURE MAP

Imagine a tropical island with sandy beaches, swaying palm trees, thick forests and high mountains. Imagine too, that somewhere on the island you have hidden a fortune in buried treasure. When you have a picture of the island in your head you can make a map of the island to show where the treasure is buried. Look at a map of a real island for ideas. Here is one way of making the map.

You will need: ● thin card ● a pencil ● plain paper ● glue ● scissors ● coloured pens or pencils

1. You can make your map as large or small as you like. The one shown here is about 40 cm by 60 cm. It was made by joining four sheets of A4 paper with sticky tape.

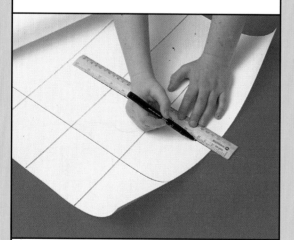

▲ **2.** Before you start drawing, decide the scale of the map. This map uses a scale of 10 cm on the map for each kilometre on the island. Draw a grid on your map with lines every 0.5 kilometres (5cm on the map).

▲ **3.** In pencil, sketch the coastline of your island on the paper. Also sketch rocks and coral reefs in the sea. When you have finalised the shape, draw the coastline in blue pen.

▲ **4.** Now decide where to put hills and mountains, rivers, lakes, forests, beaches and cliffs. Design picture symbols for all these features and sketch them on your map in pencil. When you are happy with them, colour them in.

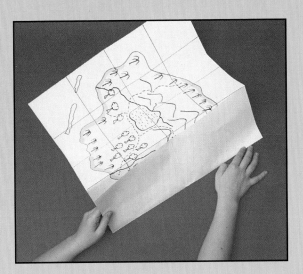

5. Finish your map by adding a key to the symbols you have used. Remember to draw a scale as well. Fold the map carefully.

6. Finally, make a case for your map. Cut one piece of card slightly bigger than the folded map. Cut another piece slightly bigger than the first. Fold the edges of the second piece around the edges of the first and glue them down. Decorate the case.

MOUNTAINS
RIVERS
LAKES
FOOTPATHS
TREES
PALM TREES
BEACH
CLIFFS
BURIED TREASURE

0   ½   1
km

MAP HISTORY

Today the whole world has been measured and mapped. However, just a hundred years ago many places were still unmapped. Five hundred years ago, European maps of the world did not show the Americas or Australia because the map-makers did not realise they existed.

THE FIRST MAPS

The oldest map we know of was made in about 2300 B.C. in Mesopotamia, which is now part of Iraq. The map was carved in a block of clay. The Greeks and the Chinese made maps of the parts of the world they knew about. In about 150 A.D. a Greek geographer called Ptolemy wrote down all he knew about maps and map-making in a famous book called *Geography*.

A map of the world according to Ptolemy (above)

IMAGINARY MAPS

Unfortunately, map-making got worse until the 1400s. Medieval map-makers drew what they imagined the world looked like. They drew the Earth as a round shape, but they did not know what it was really like. The countries and continents were the wrong shapes and in the wrong places. Some maps showed the world surrounded by a huge river called the Oceanus.

This map of the world is called the Mappa Mundi. It was drawn in the 13th century.

BETTER MAPS

Maps started to get more realistic and more accurate in the 1400s. Explorers and traders began to travel across the oceans finding new routes and new lands. They had just started to use the compass, so they could work out where they were. They made maps of the coastlines they found. When the explorers returned home the new information was added to maps. The invention of the printing press meant that maps could be copied more easily than when they had been drawn by hand. By 1800, there were accurate instruments for working out a ship's position on the Earth's surface. People began to make accurate maps of land regions as well as coasts.

MAPS FROM THE AIR

Soon after the first aeroplane flew, in 1903, map-makers started taking photographs of the ground below. This made map-making much quicker and more accurate. Most modern maps have been made using information from aerial photographs. The latest development in map-making is the use of computers to store all the information needed to draw a map.

MAPPING THE WORLD

The Earth is shaped like a slightly squashed sphere. Making a map of the Earth is difficult because you cannot draw the surface on a piece of paper without some areas being out of shape on the map.

THE POLES AND EQUATOR

The Earth spins around an imaginary line called its axis. The points on the Earth's surface at each end of the axis are called the North Pole and the South Pole. An imaginary line around the middle of the Earth half way between the poles is called the Equator. The Equator divides the Earth into two parts, called the northern hemisphere and the southern hemisphere.

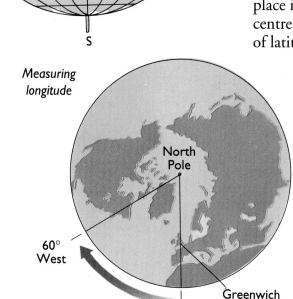

LATITUDE AND LONGITUDE

The position of a place on the Earth's surface is measured by its latitude and longitude. Latitude and longitude are measured in angles, not in kilometres. Longitude is a measure of how far around the Earth a place is (starting from Greenwich in England and going to the east or to the west). Latitude is a measure of how far north or south of the Equator the place is. The angles are measured from the Earth's centre. A map has lines on it showing the degrees of latitude and longitude.

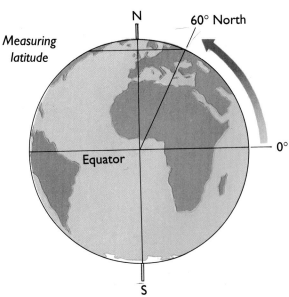

MAP PROJECTIONS

To draw a map of the world, you have to imagine the Earth's surface unfolded and laid out flat, like peeling an orange. This is called a map projection. There are many different types of map projections. Each one makes the countries look slightly different in shape and size.

A Mercator projection is used for sea charts. It makes the lines of latitude and longitude straight on the map, but the further north and south you go, the more stretched and distorted the map gets. Greenland looks much bigger than it really is.

Mercator projection (above)

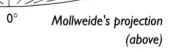

Mollweide's projection (above)

Mollweide's projection makes the countries look the right size compared to each other. Remember that the areas on the far left and far right are actually next to each other in real life.

GLOBES

A globe is a map of the world drawn on a sphere. A globe is the only sort of map that shows the countries and continents in their correct place and the right size and shape. You can find out more about globes on pages 18-19.

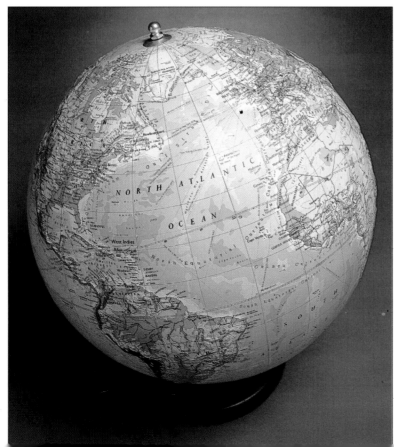

17

MAKE A PAPER GLOBE

A globe is the only sort of map that can show the whole world with all the countries in their correct position and the right shape and size. Here's how to make a globe from paper.

You will need: ● tracing paper ● cartridge paper (or thin card) ● scissors ● paper ● thick card ● coloured pens or pencils ● thin wooden dowelling

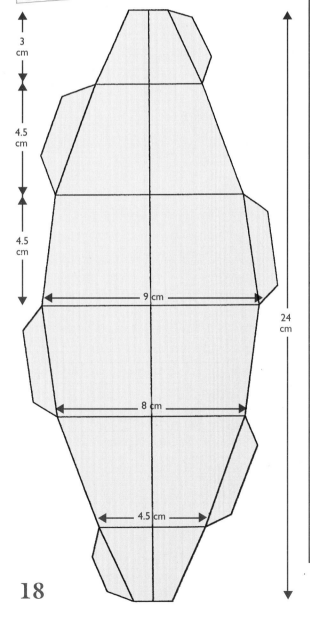

3 cm

4.5 cm

4.5 cm

9 cm

8 cm

4.5 cm

24 cm

▲ **1.** Copy the template on the left on to tracing paper. Lay the tracing paper on a sheet of cartridge paper. Push a drawing pin through the tracing paper to make marks in the cartridge paper where the lines on the template start and finish.

2. In pencil, join the holes you have made to produce a copy of the template. Make six copies in total. Draw over all the lines with a black pen and cut out the shapes. Using a ruler and the point of a pair of scissors, score along the lines.

▲ **3.** Lay the six shapes side by side. Now copy the world map shown on the right on to the shapes. Use the lines on the map and the shapes to help you get the countries in the right places.

▲ **4.** Put glue on the flaps on one edge of two of the shapes. Interlock the flaps to join the shapes together. Add another shape to these. Keep going until all six pieces are joined together.

▲ **5.** Cut two circles of card to cover the holes in the top and bottom of the globe. Using a sharp pencil, pierce a hole in the middle of each one. Glue the circles in place. Have a piece of dowelling cut, long enough to fit through the globe as its axis (see page 16) and stick out about 5 cm at each end.

6. Finish the globe by cutting a base from thick card. Fold it in half and stick the bottom of the dowelling into the fold to stand the globe up.

INFORMATION ON MAPS

A particular area can have many different types of map. For example, a map of Europe could show the borders between the different countries, the road and railway network, the crops that are grown in each country, or what the landscape is like.

Relief map

Contour map

PHYSICAL MAPS

A physical map shows what the landscape is like. It shows hills and mountains, rivers and lakes, forests and deserts. Contour lines are used to show how the land rises and falls in hills, mountains and valleys. Each line joins up places of the same height. On some maps the areas between the contours are shaded. Many physical maps also show the man-made features on the landscape, such as towns, roads and railways.

POLITICAL MAPS

A political map shows how the world is divided up into countries or regions. For example, a political map of the world shows the outline of every country of the world. The countries can be shaded in different colours. It might also show the capital city of each country.

Political map of Europe (right)

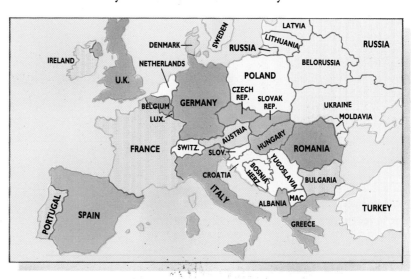

CLIMATE

The climate of a place describes what the weather is normally like there during the year. For example, the climate in western Europe is warm and dry in the summer and cold and wet in the winter. Climate maps normally show the average rainfall and average temperature during January and July.

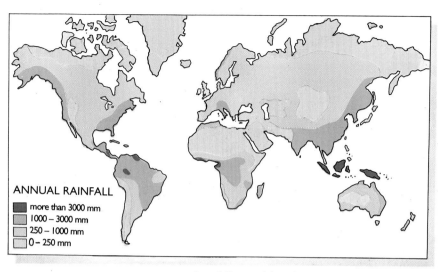

ANNUAL RAINFALL

- more than 3000 mm
- 1000 – 3000 mm
- 250 – 1000 mm
- 0 – 250 mm

Rainfall map (above)

Coal resource map (left)

COAL PRODUCTION

RESOURCES MAP

A resources map shows what sort of natural or agricultural resources, such as crops or minerals, there are in a certain area. The amount of a resource is shown by a picture symbol. The bigger the symbol, the more of the resource there is.

ROAD MAP

A road map is designed to make finding a route as easy as possible. The roads are brightly coloured and clearly numbered. Because road maps are often used by tourists, places of interest, such as castles and battlefields, are shown by special symbols.

MAKE A 3-D RELIEF MAP

You can make a contour map that is actually shaped like the landscape. After building up the shape, you can paint on features such as forest and rivers.

You will need: ● craft knife ● pencil ● newspaper ● plain paper ● paints ● thick cardboard for a base (about 30 cm x 30 cm square) ● wallpaper paste (fungicide free) ● polystyrene

▲ **1.** Start with a sheet of plain paper (A4 or larger). Design simple hills and valleys by drawing contour lines on the paper. Start with contours to represent low heights and work up to the tops of the hills.

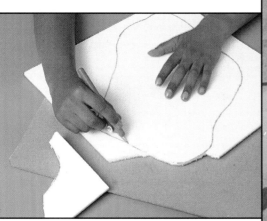

▲ **2.** Cut around the lowest contour on your map. Lay the shape on a piece of polystyrene and draw around it. Using a craft knife, carefully cut this shape out.

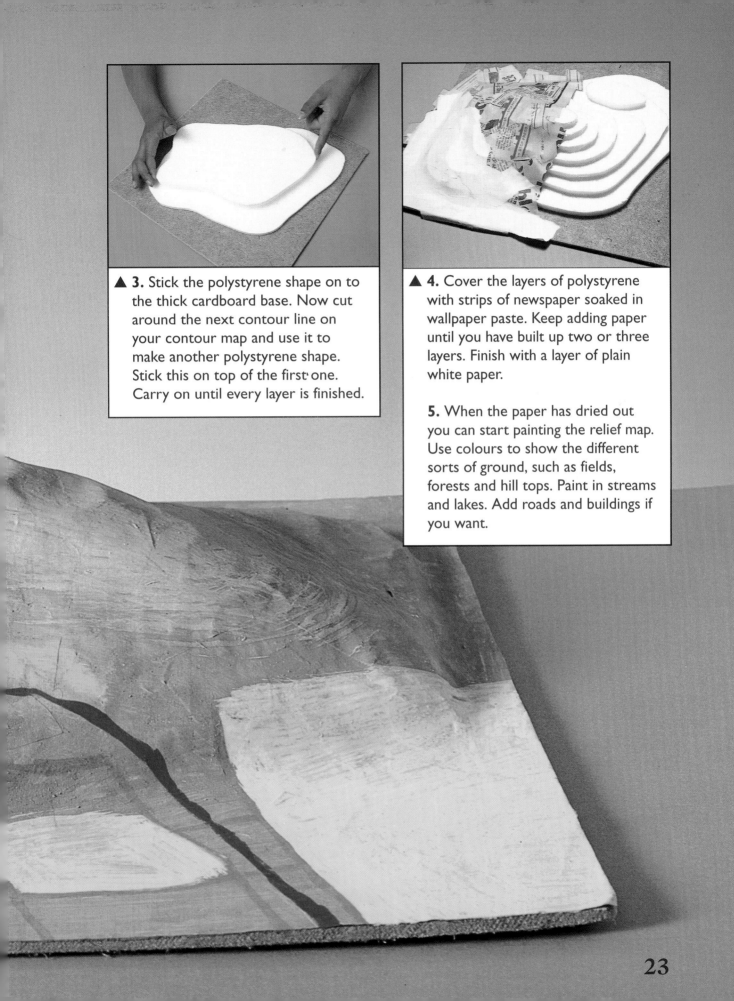

▲ **3.** Stick the polystyrene shape on to the thick cardboard base. Now cut around the next contour line on your contour map and use it to make another polystyrene shape. Stick this on top of the first one. Carry on until every layer is finished.

▲ **4.** Cover the layers of polystyrene with strips of newspaper soaked in wallpaper paste. Keep adding paper until you have built up two or three layers. Finish with a layer of plain white paper.

5. When the paper has dried out you can start painting the relief map. Use colours to show the different sorts of ground, such as fields, forests and hill tops. Paint in streams and lakes. Add roads and buildings if you want.

USING MAPS

You can use a map to find your way from place to place or to look up information about the landscape around you. Before you can plan a route, you need to work out your position on the map, then match the directions on the map with the directions on the ground.

FINDING YOUR PLACE

To find your position on the map, look for a landmark such as a church or a road junction. Then match the real landmark with the landmark on the map. Study the map and check that it matches the other features around you.

WHICH WAY?

Once you know where you are, you need to work out which direction you are looking in and turn the map round so it matches the ground. This is called orientating the map. This is quite easy if you are on a road or path. However, if there were no landmarks you would need to use a compass . Turn the map until the symbol on the map which shows magnetic north lines up with the compass needle. Now the directions on the map are the same as in real life.

HOW FAR?

You can work out how far it is along a route from one place to another by looking at the scale. Use a map measurer like the one on page 9 to work out the distance accurately, or make a rough estimate. Road maps show the distances between large towns and major road junctions with numbers written next to the road.

USING THE GRID

The position of a landmark can be given by using the grid on a map. The index of an atlas or street plan gives the position of towns and cities by indicating which page and grid square it is on. On maps which have a grid with letters and numbers, positions are given by the letter first, then the number. This is called a grid reference. Other maps have a grid with latitude and longitude numbers marked, like a graph. Here a position can be given by specifying the latitude and longitude numbers of the point.

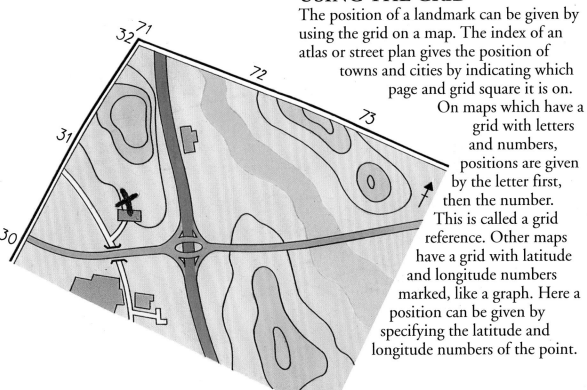

SPECIAL MAPS

Most maps show the surface of the Earth. However, there are many other sorts of map. There are maps for special uses, such as navigating at sea, and maps of special places, such as the bottom of the oceans and the surface of the Moon.

CHARTS

A chart is a map used for navigation. The most usual type is a marine chart, used on board ships. Marine charts show the position of lighthouses, buoys and wrecks, plus other navigational information. They also show the depth of the water and the position of dangerous sandbanks so that ships can avoid going aground. The grid on a chart is made up of lines of latitude and longitude. The scale shows nautical miles which are the unit of distance used at sea. One nautical mile equals 1.8 km on the ground. Aeronautical charts are used by pilots. They show airport details, radio beacons and navigational information.

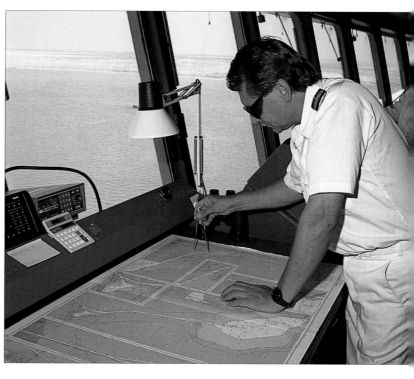

MAPS FOR ASTRONOMERS

Astronomers use maps showing the position of the stars and constellations (groups of stars). These maps are called star charts. Star charts are a bit like maps of the Earth. Some parts have to be stretched to fit the chart on a flat piece of paper. The only way to show the stars properly is by drawing the chart on the inside of a sphere.

A Planetarium shows stars by projecting a chart on to the inside of a large dome.

OCEANOGRAPHIC CHARTS

An oceanographic chart is a relief map of the bottom of the seas and oceans. Scientists use sound-measuring instruments called sonar to measure the depth of the sea. The sonar sends a pulse of sound down into the sea. The sound bounces off the seabed and back again. The deeper the sea, the longer the sound takes to get back up to the ship.

COMPUTERISED MAPS

Road map software can be used to make a computer calculate the best route between two places. The computer stores information about all the roads and how they connect together. It can work out the shortest route or the fastest route and print directions for a motorist to use on a journey.

SHINING STAR MAP

You will need: ● cardboard box
● scissors ● craft knife ● tracing paper
● thin card ● a star chart ● pins
● sticky tape

▲ **1.** Stick down any loose flaps on the cardboard box. Using a craft knife, carefully cut two holes in opposite sides of the box. Cut a piece of tracing paper large enough to cover one of the holes and stick it in place. Cut a piece of thin card large enough to cover the other hole.

3. Put the star chart tracing over the thin card. Make a tiny hole for each star by pushing a pin through the tracing paper and the card. Finally, stick the card over the second hole in the box. Hold the box up to the light to see the star chart.

2. Lay tracing paper over the star chart and trace the positions of some of the star constellations.

TOPOLOGICAL MAPS

Many maps show things on the ground in their right places and at the correct size in relationship to each other. Sometimes, however, such details are not important. For example, a map showing railway routes between towns and cities does not need to show the bends in the railway track. It just needs to show how the towns are connected. This sort of map is called a topological map.

Another example of a topological map is a motorway map. When you are in a car on a motorway, you do not need to know how the motorway twists and turns. You just need to know where to turn off, so a motorway map can be drawn with straight lines.

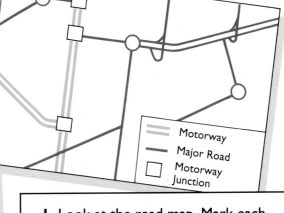

	Motorway
	Major Road
□	Motorway Junction

●	Stations
	Southern Line
	Central Line
	Northern Line
	Western Line

WOOLLY ROAD MAP

You will need: ● drawing pins ● road map ● different coloured wool ● wood or cork baseboard

1. Look at the road map. Mark each big town or large road junction by pushing a drawing pin into the baseboard. Use a different coloured wool for each type of road (motorways, major and minor roads). Tie the strands of wool around the drawing pins to connect the big towns and junctions.

GLOSSARY

Chart – A special type of map used for navigation. Marine charts are used by sailors. Aeronautical charts are used by pilots.

Contour – A line on a contour map which joins up points of equal height above mean sea level (see below).

Equator – An imaginary line around the middle of the Earth.

Hemisphere – Half of a sphere. For map-making purposes, we imagine the Earth is divided into two hemispheres (the Southern Hemisphere and the Northern Hemisphere) by the Equator.

Key – A list on a map, showing what the symbols on the map mean.

Latitude – The position of a point on the Earth, measured in degrees north or south from the Equator.

Longitude – The position of a point on the Earth, measured in degrees east or west from an imaginary line between the poles running through Greenwich, England.

Magnetic north – The point on the Earth's surface toward which the north pole of a magnet points if allowed to swing freely.

Mean sea level – The average level of the sea during the year. Mean sea level is used as a base when measuring the height of points on land.

Oceanography – The study of the sea.

Plan – A large-scale map of a small area of land.

Poles – The two points (called the North Pole and South Pole) at each end of the Earth's axis.

Political map – A map showing political information, such as the boundaries between countries and capital cities.

Projection – A way of showing the curved surface of the Earth on a flat sheet of paper.

Relief map – A map showing how the land rises and falls in hills and valleys.

Scale – The size of objects on a map compared to their actual size.

Theodolite – A device used by surveyors to measure angles accurately.

Topographic map – A map showing the physical features (natural and man-made) on the Earth's surface, such as roads, lakes, rivers and buildings.

Topological map – A map showing how places are linked together, for example, by roads or railways.

RESOURCES

MATERIALS
Most of the items used in the projects in this book can be obtained from craft shops, artists' materials shops or large stationery stores.

PLACES TO VISIT
The places listed below have exhibitions related to maps, or collections of maps. In addition, most local museums and libraries will have maps of the local area, as well as national and international maps and atlases. To find out where your local museums are, contact your local tourist information centre.

The London Planetarium
Marylebone Road
London NW1 5LA
Tel: 0171 486 1121

The Old Observatory (this stands on the Greenwich Meridian)
Greenwich Park
London SE10 8XJ
Tel: 0181 858 1167

Stanfords (the world's largest map shop)
12-14 Long Acre
London WC2E 9LP
Tel: 0171 836 1915

Map Library
British Library
Great Russell Street
London WC1B 3DG

BOOKS TO READ

Discover Maps by Patricia and Steve Harrison (Collins)

Follow the Map by John Wilson and Ordance Survey (A & C Black)

Maps and Journeys by Kate Petty (A & C Black)

Master Maps by Patricia and Steve Harrison (Collins)

Our Globe, Our Globe by Kate Petty (A & C Black)

Most children's atlases will contain information about maps. Look in your local library.

Index

Additional photographs:
Ancient Art & Architecture Collection 14 (both); Eye Ubiquitous © Gavin Wickham 15; Robert Harding Picture Library 26 (t); Angelo Hornack 11(both); The London Planetarium 26 (b); Portfolio Pictures 5; Tony Stone Images © Dan Bosler 21; ZEFA 17.